CLB 2633
Published 1995 by CLB Publishing
Exclusively for Selecta Book Ltd, Devizes
© 1991 CLB Publishing, Godalming, Surrey
ISBN 1-85833-313-X

Printed and bound in Singapore

Microwave
Healthy Eating

SELECT
EDITIONS

Microwave Healthy Eating

We are all becoming more health conscious. Even the most traditional among us are beginning to look for healthier ways of eating. This is one of the ways a microwave oven can help out in the kitchen. A microwave oven is of benefit because it turns out healthier meals in double-quick time.

Food cooked in a microwave oven retains all its natural moisture and goodness, so chicken and fish will be tender, juicy and tasty. Vegetables need less water for cooking, so they keep their crisp texture, vibrant colour and, most importantly, their vitamins. Cooking by microwaves brings out all the natural flavours of foods, so you'll find you need less salt, which is, of course, another health asset.

While some of the recipes in this chapter use classic health foods such as lentils and other dried pulses, they also use ingredients your family already enjoys; nothing unusual, just good, wholesome foods like fresh vegetables and fruit, protein-rich fish and chicken, and pasta and rice.

All microwave recipes were prepared in a 700 watt oven. If your microwave is of a lower output, adjust timings as follows:

500 watt – add 40 seconds for every minute stated in the recipe
600 watt – add 20 seconds for every minute stated in the recipe
650 watt – only a slight increase in the overall time is necessary

GINGERED SWEDE

SERVES 4

Swede, sometimes watery when boiled, is light and fluffy when cooked in a microwave oven.

450g/1lb swede, peeled
4 tbsps water
Sea salt
Freshly ground black pepper
15g/½oz low fat spread
2 tbsps fresh ginger, peeled and grated
Fresh ginger, peeled and cut into thin strips, or
    parsley, to garnish

Step 1 Place the small pieces of swede in a bowl with the water and seasoning.

1. Cut the swede into small pieces and place in a bowl with the water, sea salt and freshly ground black pepper.

2. Loosely cover and cook on HIGH for 10-15 minutes or until tender, stirring twice.

3. Drain well and mash thoroughly or purée in a

Step 2 Loosely cover the bowl with cling film, leaving a gap for the steam to escape.

food processor with the low fat spread. Stir in the ginger.

4. Reheat on HIGH for 1-2 minutes if necessary. Serve hot. Garnish with fresh ginger or parsley.

Step 3 Mash the well-drained swede with the low fat spread until smooth.

Cook's Notes

 TIME: Preparation takes about 10 minutes, and cooking takes 11-17 minutes.

 VARIATION: Combine with parsnips for a slightly different taste. Cook at the same time as the swede.

 SERVING IDEAS: Serve with any roast meat or poultry.

CREAMY BEANS
SERVES 4

*This vegetable recipe with its delicious creamy sauce makes an
excellent and very quick side dish.*

450g/1lb fresh or frozen green beans, topped and
    tailed
½ tsp grated nutmeg
Pinch sea salt
30g/1oz toasted sliced almonds
120ml/4 fl oz low fat natural yogurt

If using fresh beans,
top and tail them first.

1. Cook the beans in a covered casserole for 3
minutes on HIGH in 2 tbsps water if fresh, or for
5-10 minutes on HIGH, with no additional water, if
frozen.

2. Sprinkle on the nutmeg, sea salt and almonds.

Step 2 Combine the
beans with the
nutmeg, sea salt and
almonds.

Step 3 Make sure the
beans are very hot
before adding the
yogurt.

3. Mix in the low fat natural yogurt. Serve
immediately.

Cook's Notes

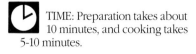 TIME: Preparation takes about
10 minutes, and cooking takes
5-10 minutes.

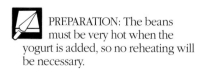 PREPARATION: The beans
must be very hot when the
yogurt is added, so no reheating will
be necessary.

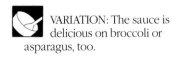 VARIATION: The sauce is
delicious on broccoli or
asparagus, too.

ROSEMARY LYONNAISE POTATOES

SERVES 4

This potato dish cooks in less than half the time it would need in a regular oven.

450g/1lb potatoes
30g/1oz low fat spread
1 tbsp finely chopped rosemary
1 small clove garlic, crushed
1 small onion, finely chopped
2 tbsps skimmed milk
Sea salt
Freshly ground black pepper

1. Peel and thinly slice the potatoes.

2. Put the low fat spread, rosemary, garlic and onions in a 20cm/8-inch, shallow dish and cook on HIGH for 3 minutes until soft.

3. Stir in the skimmed milk, sea salt and freshly ground black pepper and add the potatoes

Step 2 Soften the onion, garlic and rosemary in the low fat spread.

arranging them neatly in the dish.

4. Cover and cook on MEDIUM for 12-15 minutes until the potatoes are soft. Brown under a grill if desired.

Step 1 Slice the potatoes thinly and evenly with a food processor or mandoline.

Step 3 Add the potatoes to the other ingredients and arrange them neatly in the dish.

Cook's Notes

 TIME: Preparation takes about 10 minutes, and cooking takes 12-15 minutes.

 VARIATION: Other herbs can be substituted for rosemary. Chopped, cooked ham can be added and the dish served as a light supper or lunch.

 SERVING IDEAS: Serve with roast chicken or lamb as a change from roast potatoes. It is also good with gammon or pork.

CABBAGE WITH CARAWAY

SERVES 4

*Vegetables cooked in a microwave oven retain all their fresh flavour
and colour and their crispy texture too.*

450g/1lb green cabbage
4 tbsps water
Sea salt
30g/1oz low fat spread
2 tbsps caraway seeds
Freshly ground black pepper

Step 1 Place the finely shredded cabbage in a roasting bag with the sea salt and water.

Step 2 Use string or a non-metallic tie to secure the bag and place it on an oven turntable.

Step 4 In a bowl, toss the cooked cabbage with the low fat spread and caraway seeds.

1. Finely shred the cabbage and place in a roasting bag with the sea salt and water.

2. Tie loosely and cook on HIGH for 5-6 minutes until cooked but still slightly crisp. Drain well.

3. Place the low fat spread in a large bowl and cook on HIGH for 1 minute or until melted.

4. Add the caraway seeds and pepper and stir well. Add the cooked cabbage and toss. Serve garnished with extra caraway seeds if desired.

Cook's Notes

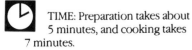 TIME: Preparation takes about 5 minutes, and cooking takes 7 minutes.

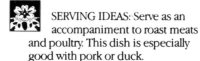 SERVING IDEAS: Serve as an accompaniment to roast meats and poultry. This dish is especially good with pork or duck.

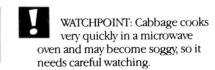 WATCHPOINT: Cabbage cooks very quickly in a microwave oven and may become soggy, so it needs careful watching.

SUCCOTASH

SERVES 4

This colourful dish was named by the American Indians. Updated, it cooks beautifully in a microwave oven.

450g/1lb butter beans
1 medium onion, chopped
1 green pepper, chopped
30g/1oz low fat spread
450g/1lb frozen sweetcorn
120ml/4 fl oz low fat natural yoghurt
1 tsp arrowroot

1. To cook the beans in the microwave, pour over boiling water to cover and allow to soak for at least 2 hours, or follow the instructions in the Cook's Tip below for rehydrating pulses.

2. Drain and cover with fresh water. Microwave on HIGH for 10 minutes and then on MEDIUM for 1 hour or until soft.

3. Combine the onions and pepper with the low fat spread, and microwave for 2 minutes on HIGH.

4. Add the cooked beans and the frozen sweetcorn and microwave for 4 minutes on HIGH.

5. Mix the arrowroot into 1 tbsp of the yoghurt, then add the rest of the yoghurt. Stir into the beans and sweetcorn before serving.

Step 1 Soak the beans until they swell in size.

Step 4 Combine the cooked beans, peppers and onion with the frozen corn and cook until the corn has defrosted and heated through.

Step 5 Mix the arrowroot with the yoghurt and stir it into the vegetables.

Cook's Notes

TIME: Preparation takes about 1 hour, to rehydrate the beans. Cooking takes about 1 hour.

SERVING IDEAS: Succotash is often served with bacon, but if you don't eat meat try it with a tomato dish.

PREPARATION: Although cooking dried pulses in a microwave oven takes almost as long as boiling them, they will have a much better texture with less chance of breaking up.

COOK'S TIP: To eliminate overnight soaking of dried pulses, cover them with water in a large bowl and heat on HIGH for about 10 minutes or until boiling. Allow to boil for about 2 minutes and then leave to stand for 1 hour.

HEARTY PEA SOUP

SERVES 6

This filling soup is a healthy family favourite. Sausages add extra flavour.

450g/1lb split peas
1.7 litres/3 pints boiling water or stock
2 leeks, sliced
2 medium onions, sliced
1 stalk celery, sliced
2 large carrots, sliced
225g/8oz thickly sliced bacon, diced
1 large smoked sausage, thickly sliced or 225g/8oz
    frankfurters or saveloys, thickly sliced
Sea salt and freshly ground black pepper
Low fat natural yoghurt

1. To cook the split peas in the microwave, cover them with boiling water and leave to soak for at least 1 hour.

2. Drain, place them in a large casserole and pour

Step 3 Add the bacon and chopped vegetables to the peas and cook until the vegetables soften.

over 850ml/1½ pints of the boiling water or stock. Microwave for 15 minutes on HIGH, or until the peas are soft.

3. Purée half of the cooked peas and return them to the casserole. Add the chopped vegetables, diced bacon and the rest of the boiling water or stock and microwave for 20 minutes on HIGH, or until the vegetables are soft.

Step 4 Add the sausages to the soup mixture and continue cooking.

4. Add the thickly sliced smoked sausage, frankfurters or saveloys, season to taste with salt and pepper, and microwave for a further 5 minutes on HIGH.

5. Leave to stand for at least 15 minutes before serving. Top each serving with a spoonful of yoghurt.

Cook's Notes

TIME: Preparation takes about 20 minutes, plus 1 hour to soak the peas. Cooking takes about 40 minutes.

SERVING IDEAS: Serve this hearty soup with chunks of fresh wholemeal bread or rolls for a complete, warming winter supper.

FREEZING: Allow the soup to cool completely. Pour into rigid containers, seal, label and freeze for up to 3 months. Reheat using DEFROST or LOW settings and break up the soup as it defrosts.

LENTIL VEGETABLE SOUP
SERVES 4

_For convenience this soup can be prepared in advance. It will taste
even better reheated as the flavours will have had a chance to develop._

450g/1lb green or brown lentils
1.2 litres/2½ pints boiling water or stock
1 bacon or ham bone (optional)
3 medium carrots, sliced
2 leeks, sliced
½ small cabbage, shredded
1 bay leaf
570ml/1 pint additional water
½ tsp dried sage
1 tsp sea salt

Step 3 Transfer half the lentils and their cooking liquid and purée until smooth.

1. To microwave the lentils, pour over boiling water and allow them to soak for at least 15 minutes.

2. Drain, then cover them with fresh boiling water or stock and microwave on HIGH for 15-20 minutes, or until they are soft.

3. Purée half of the cooked lentils with the cooking liquid. Add the remaining lentils, the bacon or ham bone, if using, the vegetables, herbs, remaining water and salt.

4. Microwave on HIGH for 10-15 minutes, or until all the vegetables are cooked.

Step 4 Test the vegetables after 10 minutes. If they cut easily, they are sufficiently well cooked.

5. Allow to stand for at least 15 minutes before serving, to allow the flavours to blend.

Cook's Notes

 TIME: Preparation takes about 15 minutes, and cooking takes 25-30 minutes.

VARIATION: You can vary the vegetables as you wish. Leave out the bacon or ham bone if you wish to make a vegetarian soup.

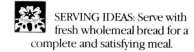 SERVING IDEAS: Serve with fresh wholemeal bread for a complete and satisfying meal.

MACARONI IN TOMATO-YOGHURT SAUCE

SERVES 4

For a quick supper dish made from store cupboard ingredients, this dish can't be bettered.

30g/1oz dried mushrooms
1 tbsp sunflower oil
1 medium onion, sliced
1 clove garlic, crushed
120ml/4 fl oz tomato juice
1 tsp dried mixed herbs
1½ tsps dried basil
850ml/1½ pints hot water or vegetable stock
225g/8oz wholemeal macaroni or wholemeal pasta
120ml/4 fl oz low fat natural yoghurt
Sea salt and freshly ground black pepper to taste

1. Rinse the mushrooms well to remove any grit, then pour boiling water over and leave them to soak while you prepare the sauce.

2. Cook the onion and garlic in the oil for 2 minutes on HIGH.

3. Stir in the tomato juice and herbs, then mix in the water or stock.

4. Drain the mushrooms, remove stalks, slice the

Step 4 Add the uncooked macaroni to the sauce, stirring well to coat it thoroughly.

caps and add to the liquid, then stir in the uncooked macaroni. Partially cover and microwave for 10 minutes.

5. Stir occasionally during the cooking time to prevent the pasta from sticking together.

6. Allow to stand for 5 minutes, covered, to finish cooking. The pasta should be al dente. Just before serving, season to taste and stir in the low fat natural yoghurt.

Step 1 Soak the dried mushrooms until they soften and swell in size.

Step 6 Leave to stand for 5 minutes for pasta to finish cooking. Stir in the yoghurt.

Cook's Notes

TIME: Preparation takes 15 minutes, and cooking takes about 12 minutes.

PREPARATION: Pasta takes almost as long to microwave as it does to cook conventionally, but it cooks without sticking, and because it finishes cooking during standing time, there is little chance of overcooking.

VARIATION: Use any of the many small pasta shapes available to make this quick and easy vegetarian supper. Green or red pastas are good, too.

SPINACH RISOTTO

SERVES 4

For a quick supper after a busy day, a risotto is the perfect dish and economical, too.

30g/1oz low fat spread
340g/12oz brown rice
1 onion, thinly sliced
850ml/1½ pints hot vegetable stock
60g/2oz walnuts, roughly chopped
300g/10oz frozen chopped spinach, thawed, or
   300g/10oz fresh spinach, washed and chopped
60g/2oz Parmesan cheese, grated
Sea salt and freshly ground black pepper to taste

1. Melt the low fat spread on HIGH for 1 minute, then add the rice and sliced onion.

2. Stir to coat, and microwave for 2 minutes on HIGH.

3. Add the hot stock, partially cover and cook on HIGH for 30-35 minutes, or until the rice is just soft.

Step 1 Stir the rice and onion into the low fat spread before cooking.

Step 3 Add the stock and cook until the rice is just soft.

4. Stir in the walnuts and spinach and microwave for a further 5 minutes on HIGH.

Step 4 Add the walnuts and spinach and cook for a further 5 minutes.

5. Mix in the Parmesan cheese and season to taste just before serving.

Cook's Notes

 TIME: Preparation takes 15 minutes, and cooking takes 25-30 minutes.

SERVING IDEAS: Serve as an accompaniment to grilled meat, poultry or fish. For a vegetarian meal, serve with a fresh tomato salad.

BOSTON BAKED BEANS

SERVES 4

An American favourite made quick and easy with the help of canned beans and your microwave oven.

2 tbsps sunflower oil
1 large onion, sliced
450g/1lb belly of pork skinned and diced into
    4cm/1½-inch cubes
2 tbsps tomato ketchup
3 tbsps soft brown sugar
1 tsp mustard powder
1 tbsp malt vinegar
1 tbsp black treacle
425g/15oz canned haricot beans
1 tbsp cornflour mixed with a little water
Sea salt and freshly ground black pepper

4. Drain the beans, reserving 140ml/¼ pint of the liquid. Add the reserved bean liquid and the ketchup mixture to the pork. Stir well. Cover and cook on MEDIUM for 15 minutes.

Step 4 Add the sauce ingredients to the pork, mixing well.

5. Add the beans, cornflour and water and seasoning. Cook on HIGH for 5 minutes. Leave the casserole for 5-10 minutes before serving.

Step 5 Add the beans and cornflour and cook until the sauce thickens and clears.

Step 2 Cook the pork for about 3 minutes or until it loses its pink colour.

1. Pour the sunflower oil into a large casserole dish and heat on HIGH for 2 minutes. Add the onion and cook on HIGH for a further 2 minutes.

2. Add the pork and cook on HIGH for 3 minutes.

3. Mix the ketchup, sugar, mustard, vinegar and treacle together.

Cook's Notes

TIME: Preparation takes 15 minutes, and cooking takes about 27 minutes. The casserole should stand for 5-10 minutes before serving to complete cooking.

VARIATION: If desired, the pork may be omitted. Alternatively, bacon or ham may be substituted.

BUYING GUIDE: Haricot beans are usually available in supermarkets, but other varieties such as butter or white kidney beans can be used instead.

RED BEANS AND RICE

SERVES 4

*Spicy, without being hot, this combination of beans and rice makes a
colourful meal that can be prepared in advance and reheated.*

225g/8oz dried kidney beans
1 medium onion, finely chopped
1 stalk celery, thinly sliced
1 large clove garlic, crushed
½ tsp allspice or mixed spice
1 bay leaf
180g/6oz brown rice
430ml/¾ pint hot vegetable stock
60g/2oz black olives, pitted and sliced
120g/4oz low fat Cheddar cheese, grated
Sea salt and freshly ground black pepper

1. To cook the beans in the microwave, first pour
on boiling water to cover and allow to stand for at
least 2 hours. Drain, then cover with fresh boiling
water and microwave on HIGH for 35 minutes, or
until the beans are tender.

2. Alternatively, the beans may be cooked by any
other method.

3. Combine the cooked beans, chopped onion,

Step 3 Combine the
beans with the other
ingredients in a large
casserole and pour
over the stock.

celery, garlic, bay leaf and spices with the rice in a
casserole.

4. Pour over the boiling stock and microwave on
HIGH for 25 minutes, or until the rice is cooked
and the liquid is absorbed. Check near the end of
the cooking time and add extra liquid if necessary.

5. After the rice is cooked, stir in the olives and the
grated cheese and microwave for 1 minute on
HIGH to melt the cheese. Season to taste with salt
and pepper.

Step 1 Cook the
kidney beans until
completely soft, but
still whole.

Step 5 When the rice
has been cooked until
soft, stir in the olives
and cheese.

Cook's Notes

TIME: Preparation takes
15 minutes, and cooking takes
about 1 hour.

PREPARATION: If preparing the
dish in advance, add the cheese
just before reheating to prevent
stringiness.

COOK'S TIP: Canned beans may
be used instead of dried, but
remember that cooked beans are
approximately twice the weight and
volume of uncooked beans.

PASTA PAPRIKA

SERVES 4

*Pasta cooks very well in a microwave oven, without sticking to the
pan or steaming up the kitchen!*

340g/12oz green or wholewheat fettucini, fresh or
   dried
1 tsp sunflower oil
1 large onion, chopped
1 clove garlic, crushed
3 peppers, one green, one red and one yellow,
   seeded and sliced
1 tbsp olive oil
450g/1lb canned tomatoes, sieved
2 tsps paprika
60g/2oz Parmesan cheese, grated

Step 3 Cook the onion, garlic and peppers in a covered bowl until tender.

Step 1 Cook the pasta in a large bowl until just tender.

Step 4 Add the tomatoes and stir the sauce into the pasta.

1. Place the pasta in a large bowl, pour over boiling water to cover and add the sunflower oil. Cook for 5 minutes on HIGH, or until the pasta is just tender. If using fresh pasta, cook for only 2 minutes on HIGH.

2. Allow the pasta to stand in the water while you prepare the sauce.

3. Combine the onion, garlic and sliced peppers with the olive oil and cook for 4 minutes on HIGH.

4. Add the tomatoes and paprika. Stir this sauce into the drained pasta, sprinkle with the Parmesan cheese and cook for 4 minutes on HIGH. Serve immediately.

Cook's Notes

TIME: Preparation takes 20 minutes, and cooking takes 13 minutes.

VARIATION: Green peppers may be used in place of the red and yellow peppers although the combination of all three makes an attractive dish.

SERVING IDEAS: This dish can be served as an accompaniment to grilled chicken or fish, or as a delicious vegetarian main course with a salad and wholemeal bread.

LASAGNE ROLLS

SERVES 4

Lasagne takes on a new look when the pasta sheets are rolled around a tasty spinach filling.

225g/8oz wholewheat lasagne
1 tsp sunflower oil
340g/12oz fresh or frozen spinach, finely chopped
340g/12oz low fat cottage cheese
60g/2oz Parmesan cheese, grated
60g/2oz pine nuts
1 egg, beaten
½ tsp sea salt
225g/8oz tomato purée
180ml/6 fl oz water
2 tsps mixed herbs

1. Cook the lasagne, two or three sheets at a time, in boiling water to which you have added 1 tsp oil. Place a few sheets in the water, microwave for 1-2 minutes on HIGH, or until they are just soft, but not fully cooked.

Step 1 Cook the sheets of lasagne 2 or 3 at a time in a large bowl.

2. Set aside the cooked sheets separately to prevent them sticking together.

3. Cook the spinach for 5 minutes on HIGH with no additional water, if frozen, or 3 minutes on HIGH with a small amount of water, if fresh.

4. Drain and mix into the cottage cheese. Add the Parmesan cheese, beaten egg, pine nuts and salt and set aside.

5. Prepare a sauce by combining the tomato purée with the water and herbs.

Step 2 To prevent the lasagne sheets sticking together, spread them out on paper towels to drain.

Step 6 Place some of the cottage cheese mixture on each lasagne sheet and roll up.

6. Place a large spoonful of the cottage cheese mixture on each sheet of lasagne and roll them up. Arrange the rolls in a dish, and pour over the sauce.

7. Bake for 10 minutes on HIGH, or until the lasagne is fully cooked and most of the liquid has been absorbed. Check halfway through the cooking time and add more water if the dish seems dry.

Cook's Notes

 TIME: Preparation takes about 35 minutes, and cooking takes about 15 minutes.

 VARIATION: Tomato purée is used to make the sauce in this recipe. If desired, substitute a 400g/14oz can of tomatoes and their juice.

 BUYING GUIDE: Pine nuts are available in delicatessens or speciality food stores, but supermarkets often stock them, too. They are expensive, so any other variety of nuts can be used.

SMOKED HADDOCK AND CHIVES AU GRATIN

SERVES 4

Smoked fish combines so well with cheese and chives. Serve this for supper, lunch or even brunch.

340g/12oz smoked haddock, skinned
140ml/¼ pint white wine
1 bay leaf
120g/4oz mushrooms, sliced
30g/1oz low fat spread
30g/1oz wholemeal flour
140ml/¼ pint skimmed milk
Small bunch fresh chives, chopped
60g/2oz low fat Cheddar cheese, grated
1 tbsp chopped fresh parsley
4 tbsps wholemeal breadcrumbs

Step 4 Add the cooking liquid and the milk to the sauce. Cook until thickened, whisking frequently.

Step 2 Cook the haddock until it flakes easily.

Step 5 Add the flaked fish to the sauce.

1. Place the haddock in a shallow dish with the wine, bay leaf and mushrooms.

2. Cover and cook on HIGH for 3 minutes, or until the fish is cooked. Set aside.

3. Put the low fat spread in a small bowl and cook on HIGH for 30 seconds. Stir in the flour and cook on HIGH for 30 seconds.

4. Add the cooking liquor from the fish together with the milk and mix well. Cook on HIGH for 2-4 minutes, whisking every minute until thickened.

5. Add the mushrooms, chives and fish, flaking the fish slightly as you do so, and mix well.

6. Divide between four individual gratin dishes. Sprinkle over the cheese, parsley and breadcrumbs and cook on HIGH for 1-2 minutes or brown under the grill.

Cook's Notes

TIME: Preparation takes 10 minutes, and cooking takes 5-8 minutes.

VARIATION: Substitute smoked cod or prepare the dish with unsmoked fish.

SERVING IDEAS: Serve with a salad and wholemeal or granary bread.

FISHERMAN'S PIE

SERVES 4

Fish is low in fat and calories but high in flavour. For variety, choose a combination of fish and seafood.

450g/1lb fish and shellfish (mixture of whitefish, smoked fish, prawns and mussels)
675g/1½ lbs potatoes, peeled
30g/1oz low fat spread
4 tbsps hot skimmed milk
Sea salt and freshly ground black pepper

Sauce
30g/1oz low fat spread
30g/1oz flour
Skimmed milk
3 tbsps chopped parsley
Dash Tabasco
Sea salt and freshly ground black pepper

Glaze
1 egg, beaten with a pinch of sea salt

1. Skin the fish and remove any bones. Cut into chunks, place in a large bowl and cover with pierced cling film. Cook on HIGH for 4 minutes.

Step 3 Cut the potatoes into even-sized pieces before cooking in a covered bowl with the water.

2. Add the mussels to the bowl and cook for a further 2 minutes on HIGH. Leave to stand, covered, while preparing the potatoes.

3. Place the potatoes in a bowl with 4 tbsps water, cover and cook on HIGH for 10-12 minutes or until tender.

4. Drain well and mash with the low fat spread and hot skimmed milk until smooth. Season with salt and pepper.

5. Melt the low fat spread for the sauce in a glass measure for 30 seconds on HIGH. Stir in the flour and measure the juices from the fish. Make up to 280ml/½ pint with cold skimmed milk. Stir the skimmed milk and fish juices into the flour and low fat spread and whisk well.

6. Cook on HIGH for 6 minutes, whisking several times during cooking to prevent lumps forming. Stir in the parsley and add salt and pepper and a dash of Tabasco.

7. Arrange the fish and mussels in a casserole dish and add the prawns. Pour the sauce over the fish and smooth level.

8. Spoon or pipe the mashed potato on top in a lattice pattern. Glaze the potato with the beaten egg and cook on HIGH for 12-15 minutes, or until heated through. Brown under a preheated grill before serving.

Step 8 Using a plain piping nozzle, pipe the mashed potatoes over the fish in a lattice pattern.

Cook's Notes

TIME: Preparation takes about 15 minutes, and cooking takes about 26-28 minutes.

ECONOMY: To cut costs, leave out the shellfish and make up the weight with a more inexpensive fish.

FREEZING: Allow the pie to cool and then freeze until the potato is firm. Cover the pie well and freeze for up to 2 months. Heat the

HADDOCK AND POTATO CURRY

SERVES 4

A taste for curry is quickly satisfied with a microwave oven in the kitchen. It's less expensive than a takeaway too.

225g/8oz potatoes, peeled, if desired, and diced
45g/1½oz low fat spread
1 onion, finely chopped
1 fresh green chilli, seeded and chopped
1 tsp ground cumin
1 tsp ground coriander
2 cardamom pods
½ tsp tomato purée
Pinch turmeric
Sea salt to taste
140ml/¼ pint low fat natural yogurt
450g/1lb haddock, skinned, boned and cut into chunks
1 tbsp chopped fresh coriander or parsley
Cucumber twists

1. Place the potatoes in a bowl or roasting bag, add approximately 4 tbsps water and cook, covered, for 4 minutes on HIGH, or until soft. Drain and set aside

2. In a casserole, melt the low fat spread for 1 minute on HIGH. Stir in the onion and chilli and microwave for a further minute on HIGH.

3. Blend in the remaining spices and the tomato purée and cook for 1 more minute on HIGH.

4. Stir in the yogurt, then mix in the cooked potato and the fish, making sure they are well coated with sauce.

Step 1 A roasting bag may be used instead of a covered bowl for microwaving the potatoes.

5. Cover and cook for 5 minutes on HIGH, or until the fish is fully cooked, stirring once during the cooking time. Garnish the curry with the chopped coriander or parsley and the cucumber twists before serving.

Step 3 When the onion and chilli are soft, blend in the spices and tomato purée and cook for a further 1 minute.

Cook's Notes

 TIME: Preparation takes 20 minutes, and cooking takes 12 minutes.

 VARIATION: You can use other types of whitefish to make this flavourful curry if you wish.

SERVING IDEAS: Accompany the curry with additional low fat natural yogurt and a selection of chutneys and pickles. Serve with brown rice.

CREAMY FISH CHOWDER

SERVES 4

Soups make economical and healthy meals, whether as lunches, suppers or snacks. Fish, bacon and potatoes are a flavourful combination.

450g/1lb fish trimmings
1 bay leaf
430ml/¾ pint water
30g/1oz low fat spread, cut into pieces
90g/3oz rindless bacon, finely chopped
2 medium onions, chopped
450g/1lb potatoes, peeled and diced
280ml/½ pint skimmed milk
1 tsp thyme
½ tsp freshly grated nutmeg
Sea salt and freshly ground black pepper
450g/1lb whitefish fillets, cut into 1.25cm/½-inch chunks
140ml/¼ pint single cream
Chopped fresh parsley

1. First prepare the stock by combining the fish trimmings, bay leaf and stalks from the parsley with the water.

2. Microwave on HIGH for 5 minutes, or until boiling, then reduce the power and cook for 13 minutes on MEDIUM.

3. Strain the stock and set aside.

4. Place the chopped bacon and onion with the low fat spread in a large 3 litre/6-pint casserole with a lid and microwave on HIGH for 3 minutes, stirring occasionally.

5. Add the diced potatoes, reserved stock, skimmed milk, thyme, nutmeg and seasoning. Microwave on HIGH for 20 minutes, or until the potatoes are soft.

6. Liquidize approximately 430ml/¾ pint of the soup, then return it to the casserole. Add the chopped fish and cook for a further 5 minutes on HIGH, or until the fish is tender.

7. Stir in the single cream and heat through for 1 minute on HIGH. Ladle into bowls to serve and garnish with chopped parsley.

Step 1 Combine the fish bones and trimmings with the other stock ingredients in the largest bowl that will fit in the microwave.

Step 4 Cook the onion and bacon until they are soft but not beginning to colour.

Cook's Notes

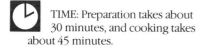

TIME: Preparation takes about 30 minutes, and cooking takes about 45 minutes.

VARIATION: For variety, try substituting smoked haddock for the whitefish or adding 60g/2oz frozen sweetcorn with the fish.

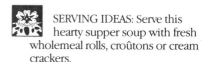

SERVING IDEAS: Serve this hearty supper soup with fresh wholemeal rolls, croûtons or cream crackers.

STUFFED PEPPERS
SERVES 4

*Peppers cook quickly in a microwave oven but retain all their taste
and texture which is very important in healthy eating.*

3 large peppers, red, yellow and green
340g/¾lb lean minced beef
1 onion, finely chopped
60g/2oz cooked brown rice
60g/2oz raisins
30g/1oz chopped walnuts
1 tbsp Worcestershire sauce
2 tsps brown sugar
2 tsps wine vinegar
Sea salt and freshly ground black pepper

Sauce
450g/1lb canned tomatoes
1 bay leaf
2 tsps chilli powder
1 clove garlic, crushed
1 tbsp tomato purée
2 tbsps cornflour mixed with 2 tbsps water
Salt and pepper

1. Cut the peppers in half and remove the cores and seeds.

2. Place them in 1 layer in a shallow dish with 4 tbsps water. Cover loosely and cook for 4 minutes on HIGH. Leave to stand, covered, while preparing the filling.

3. Cook the beef for 5-6 minutes on MEDIUM in a casserole dish.

Step 4 Cook the beef and onion, breaking it up with a fork as it cooks.

4. Add the onion and increase the setting to HIGH. Cook for another 4-6 minutes breaking the meat up with a fork frequently during cooking.

5. Stir in the rice, raisins, walnuts, Worcestershire sauce, brown sugar, vinegar and seasoning. Drain the peppers and fill with the meat mixture.

6. Combine all the sauce ingredients except the cornflour and water, in a glass measure. Cook for 12 minutes on HIGH, or until boiling.

7. Stir the cornflour and water into the sauce. Cook for a further 3 minutes, stirring frequently after 1 minute.

8. Allow to cool slightly, remove the bay leaf and purée the sauce. Strain it if desired and pour over the peppers in a serving dish. Reheat for 1-2 minutes on HIGH.

Cook's Notes

 TIME: Preparation takes about 20 minutes, and cooking takes 28-31 minutes.

 VARIATION: Many different ingredients can be added to the filling such as sweetcorn, olives, mushrooms or low fat cheese. Add to or subtract from the list of ingredients according to preference. Use 340g/12oz of cooked brown rice instead of the meat for a vegetarian filling and omit the Worcestershire sauce.

FREEZING: Cover well and freeze for up to 3 months. Defrost for 10-15 minutes on LOW or DEFROST and allow to stand for 10 minutes. Cook for 10 minutes on HIGH to reheat and serve immediately.

BRAN AND OAT MEAT LOAF

SERVES 4

The ever popular meat loaf gets a fibre boost from the addition of oats and bran. They make a pleasant change texturewise too.

450g/1lb lean minced beef
1 egg
30g/1oz bran
90g/3oz rolled oats
1 small onion, chopped
240ml/8 fl oz skimmed milk
1 tsp dried mixed herbs
1 tsp sea salt

Tomato Sauce
450g/1lb canned tomatoes
3 tbsps tomato purée
1 clove garlic, crushed
1 onion, roughly chopped
1 green pepper, diced
1 tbsp cornflour
2 tbsps cold water
Sea salt and freshly ground black pepper
Raw cane sugar (optional)

1. Mix together all the ingredients for the meat loaf and place the mixture in a loaf dish.

2. Smooth the top and cook for 15 minutes on HIGH. Leave to stand for 10 minutes before turning out.

Step 1 Mix the meat loaf ingredients together and press firmly into a loaf dish.

3. To prepare the sauce, combine the tomatoes and their juice, the purée and garlic. Cook, uncovered, on HIGH for 8 minutes or until boiling.

4. Add the onion and green pepper and cook for 5 minutes on HIGH.

Step 2 When the meat loaf is cooked, it will shrink from the edge of the dish. Leave to stand and pour off any fat.

5. Combine cornflour with the water and stir into the sauce. Cook for 3-4 minutes on HIGH, or until thickened. Season with salt and pepper and add a pinch of sugar, if desired.

6. Pour the sauce over the meat loaf and reheat, if necessary, for 2 minutes on HIGH.

Step 6 Turn the meat out onto a serving plate or board covered with aluminium foil.

Cook's Notes

TIME: Preparation takes 20 minutes, and cooking takes about 31-32 minutes.

SERVING IDEAS: Serve with chutney instead of tomato sauce, if desired. Meat loaf is particularly good served with mashed potatoes. It also makes delicious sandwiches.

LAMB COUSCOUS

SERVES 6

Couscous, a form of grain popular in North African cooking, can make meat go further and provide a lot of flavour interest.

450g/1lb lamb fillet, cut into chunks
2 onions, cut into chunks
1 clove garlic, crushed
1 green pepper, sliced
1 large potato, diced
4 carrots, sliced
2 small turnips, diced
120g/4oz dried apricots, chopped
1 tsp ground coriander
1 tsp ground cumin
1 tsp ground turmeric
1 tsp chilli powder
225g/8oz chickpeas
400g/14oz canned tomatoes, roughly chopped
450g/1lb couscous
850ml/1½ pints water
1 tsp sea salt

1. To cook the chickpeas in the microwave, pour boiling water over them and leave to soak for at least 2 hours.

2. Drain, then cook them in 1.1 litres/2 pints water for 25 minutes on HIGH.

3. Combine the lamb, onion and garlic in a casserole and cook for 5 minutes on HIGH.

4. Add the vegetables, dried apricots, spices, cooked chickpeas and tomatoes and microwave for a further 15 minutes on HIGH.

5. Set the stew aside while you prepare the

Step 4 Add the remaining stew ingredients to the precooked lamb.

Step 6 When the couscous has absorbed most of the water it will swell in size. Cook and then fluff up with a fork to separate the grains.

couscous. Place the couscous in a bowl with the salt and pour on the water.

6. Leave to stand for at least 5 minutes, until the couscous has swollen and absorbed most of the liquid. Cover the bowl and microwave on HIGH for 5 minutes. Remove the cover and fluff up the couscous with a fork. Serve the lamb on top of the couscous.

Cook's Notes

TIME: Preparation takes 25 minutes plus 2 hours to soak the chickpeas, and cooking takes 30 minutes.

VARIATION: Chicken is often served in a spicy sauce with couscous. Use chicken breasts or boned leg meat which will cook quickly.

BUYING GUIDE: More and more supermarkets and most delicatessens stock couscous. There is no real substitute, although the lamb stew is also good served with rice.

CHICKEN TOMALE BAKE

SERVES 4

The diced chicken in this dish will take about 10 minutes to microwave and will be juicy and tender.

225-450g/½-1lb cooked boneless chicken, diced
180g/6oz frozen sweetcorn
1 green pepper, chopped

Sauce
1 clove garlic, crushed
280ml/½ pint tomato juice
½ tsp ground cumin
½ tsp chilli powder
1 tsp oregano

Topping
180g/6oz polenta or corn meal
570ml/1 pint water
2 eggs
1 tsp sea salt
Pinch paprika

1. Combine the chicken and vegetables in a casserole.

2. Mix together the sauce ingredients and pour

Step 4 Beat the eggs into the cooked polenta.

over the chicken.

3. To make the topping, stir the polenta into the water and microwave on HIGH for 5 minutes.

4. Stir thoroughly then beat in the two eggs and the salt.

5. Spread the topping over the chicken and sauce mixture, sprinkle paprika on top, cover and cook for 10 minutes on HIGH, or until the topping is set.

Step 2 Combine the chicken, vegetables and sauce ingredients in a casserole.

Step 5 Spread the polenta topping carefully over the chicken and sauce.

Cook's Notes

 TIME: Preparation takes about 15 minutes, and cooking takes about 18 minutes.

 PREPARATION: This dish can be prepared ahead and refrigerated. Add 5-6 minutes to the final cooking time.

 SERVING IDEAS: This dish is almost a meal in itself, and needs only a green salad or a tomato and onion salad as an accompaniment.

CHICKEN PAPRIKA

SERVES 4

*Chicken portions are best cooked on medium for the tenderest results
and most even cooking.*

1.25kg/3¼lb chicken, cut into 8 pieces and skinned
3 tbsps sunflower oil
1 medium onion, finely sliced
1 clove garlic, crushed
1 red pepper, seeded and thinly sliced
1 tbsp mild paprika
Pinch cayenne pepper (optional)
140ml/¼ pint chicken stock
125g/8oz canned tomatoes, chopped
Sea salt and freshly ground black pepper
1 tbsp cornflour mixed with 2 tbsps cold
    water
Low fat natural yoghurt

3. Pour in the stock and tomatoes and stir well. Add the chicken and cook on MEDIUM for 30-40 minutes.

4. Blend the cornflour and the water and add to the chicken, stirring well. Cook for 6-7 minutes on MEDIUM or until the sauce thickens.

5. Allow to stand for 5 minutes. Spoon yoghurt over the top before serving, if desired.

Step 2 Add the garlic, sliced pepper, paprika and cayenne and cook for a further 2 minutes.

Step 1 Cook the onion in the oil until softened.

Step 3 Add the chicken, pushing it under the surface of the liquid as much as possible.

1. Place the sunflower oil and onion in a large casserole dish and cook on HIGH for 3 minutes.

2. Add the garlic, pepper, paprika, cayenne pepper if using and salt and pepper. Cover and cook on HIGH for 2 minutes.

Cook's Notes

 TIME: Preparation takes 20 minutes, and cooking takes 36-47 minutes with 5 minutes standing time.

SERVING IDEAS: Serve with wholewheat pasta, brown rice or boiled potatoes in their skins or jacket potatoes.

 FREEZING: Freeze in containers or in the serving dish. Cover well and store for up to 2 months. To thaw and reheat, cook uncovered on LOW or DEFROST for 15 minutes, stirring frequently. Leave to stand for 10 minutes and reheat on HIGH for 10-12 minutes. Top with low fat natural yoghurt.

SUGARLESS BAKED APPLES WITH DATES

SERVES 4

Although this recipe contains no sugar, the apples are delightfully sweet tasting. They can be eaten on their own or served with cream or yogurt.

4 large green apples
60g/2oz chopped, unsugared dates
4 tbsps sugar-free muesli
30g/1oz low fat spread
120ml/4 fl oz pure apple juice

Step 1 Use a fork or small sharp knife to prick the apple skins in several places.

Step 2 Mix together the dates and muesli and fill the cavities in the apples.

Step 3 Place the apples in a circle so that they are touching.

1. Core the apples. Prick the skins in several places, but do not peel.

2. Fill the cavities with a mixture of the muesli and dates.

3. Place the apples in a casserole so that they are touching.

4. Dot the filling with the low fat spread and pour over the apple juice. Bake for 3-4 minutes on HIGH, or until the apples are soft.

Cook's Notes

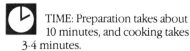
TIME: Preparation takes about 10 minutes, and cooking takes 3-4 minutes.

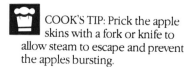
COOK'S TIP: Prick the apple skins with a fork or knife to allow steam to escape and prevent the apples bursting.

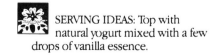
SERVING IDEAS: Top with natural yogurt mixed with a few drops of vanilla essence.

FRESH AND DRIED FRUIT SALAD

SERVES 4

Perk up dried fruit with fresh seasonal varieties — apples and oranges in winter, soft fruits or peaches in summer.

225g/8oz mixed dried fruit
240ml/8 fl oz pure apple juice
2 dessert apples
1 orange

1. Combine the dried fruit and the apple juice in a bowl and microwave on MEDIUM for 8 minutes. Allow to cool.

Step 1 Cook the dried fruit in the apple juice and leave to rehydrate.

2. Wash the orange and cut four slices to use as a garnish, then peel and roughly chop the flesh.

Step 3 Combine the chopped apple and orange with the dried fruit.

3. Wash and chop the apples, leaving the skins on. Combine the chopped apples and orange with the dried fruit and apple juice and chill.

4. To serve, divide between 4 dishes and garnish each with an orange slice.

Cook's Notes

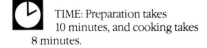

TIME: Preparation takes 10 minutes, and cooking takes 8 minutes.

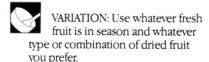

VARIATION: Use whatever fresh fruit is in season and whatever type or combination of dried fruit you prefer.

SERVING IDEAS: Serve with low fat natural yogurt or fromage frais.

SUGAR-FREE FRUIT CAKE

Makes 1 large cake

A moist and flavourful fruit cake in just over 30 minutes? Anything's possible with a microwave oven in the kitchen.

225g/8oz mixed dried fruit
330ml/11 fl oz apple juice
225g/8oz wholemeal flour
2 tsps baking powder
1 tsp mixed spice
120g/4oz low fat spread
2 eggs, beaten
Reduced sugar apricot jam

Step 2 Rub the fat into the dry ingredients until the mixture looks like fine breadcrumbs.

1. Combine the fruit and the apple juice and allow to soak for at least 1 hour.

2. Mix together the dry ingredients and rub in the butter or margarine until the mixture resembles fine breadcrumbs.

3. Beat in the eggs and mix in the fruit and juice.

4. Line the bottom of a deep 15cm/6-inch round dish with greaseproof paper. Pour in the cake mixture and smooth the top.

5. Let the mixture stand for a few minutes, then bake for 3 minutes on HIGH, followed by 13 minutes on MEDIUM, or until the centre is just dry. Allow to cool slightly, then turn out onto a rack to finish cooling.

6. When cool, brush the top with reduced sugar apricot jam.

Step 5 The centre of the cake should look dry when done.

Cook's Notes

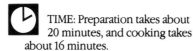
TIME: Preparation takes about 20 minutes, and cooking takes about 16 minutes.

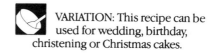
VARIATION: This recipe can be used for wedding, birthday, christening or Christmas cakes.

BANANA BRAN BREAD

Makes 1 loaf

*This teabread is the fastest ever. It also has all the goodness of bran
and wholemeal flour.*

120g/4oz low fat spread
120g/4oz muscovado sugar
2 medium eggs
2 large, very ripe bananas, mashed
4 tbsps low fat natural yoghurt
1 tsp baking powder
½ tsp baking soda
½ tsp sea salt
60g/2oz bran
180g/6oz wholemeal flour
30g/1oz toasted bran

1. Cream together the low fat spread and sugar.

2. Add the eggs, mashed bananas and low fat yoghurt.

3. Sift in the baking powder, baking soda, salt, bran and flour. Mix together thoroughly.

4. Turn the batter into a lightly greased loaf dish. Cover the top loosely with cling film and cover the corners of the dish with aluminium foil, shiny side out.

5. Cook in the microwave for 10 minutes on HIGH. Remove the foil and cling film, sprinkle on the toasted bran, replace cling film, and cook for a further 2 minutes on HIGH.

6. Remove the cling film and leave the loaf to cool in the dish for 10 minutes before turning out.

Step 3 Mix in the baking powder, baking soda, sea salt, bran and flour.

Step 1 Cream the low fat spread with the sugar until light and fluffy.

Step 4 If using a square or loaf dish, cover the corners with foil.

Cook's Notes

 TIME: Preparation takes about 20 minutes, and cooking takes about 12 minutes.

 COOK'S TIP: Covering the corners of cakes baked in square or loaf dishes prevents uneven cooking. The foil will deflect the microwaves, but use it sparingly.

 SERVING IDEAS: This teabread is particularly delicious served cold, sliced and spread with low fat cream cheese.

PEACH COBBLER CAKE

SERVES 4

This marvellous pudding is simplicity itself to prepare and it cooks in less than 15 minutes. The brown sugar topping is absolutely delicious.

15g/½oz low fat spread
30g/1oz muscovado sugar
400g/14oz canned peaches, drained
Large pinch nutmeg
30g/1oz raw cane sugar
60g/2oz bran
60g/2oz wholemeal flour
1 tsp baking powder
½ tsp cinnamon
Pinch sea salt
60g/2oz low fat spread
150ml/¼ pint skimmed milk

1. Melt 15g/½oz low fat spread in an 18cm/7-inch square or round dish for 1 minute on HIGH.

2. Stir in the muscovado sugar and spread evenly over the bottom of the dish. Arrange the peaches on top.

3. In a separate bowl mix together the dry ingredients and rub in the butter. Stir in the skimmed milk to form a soft dough.

4. Cover the peaches as evenly as possible with the mixture and bake, uncovered, for 12 minutes on HIGH, or until the centre is just cooked.

Step 2 Stir the sugar into the melted low fat spread and spread evenly over the base of the baking dish.

Step 4 Spread the cake mixture over the peaches and the sugar topping.

5. Allow to cool for 15 minutes, then invert carefully onto a plate to serve.

Cook's Notes

 TIME: Preparation takes 15 minutes, and cooking takes 12 minutes.

 SERVING IDEAS: The cake is best served warm and can be accompanied with low fat natural yoghurt.

 PREPARATION: The dish can be lined with greaseproof paper to help ease the cake out of the dish.

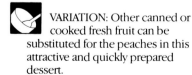 VARIATION: Other canned or cooked fresh fruit can be substituted for the peaches in this attractive and quickly prepared dessert.

FLAPJACKS

MAKES 8

These favourite family treats are low in sugar and cook in less than 5 minutes. Two good reasons for making them often.

120g/4oz low fat spread
2 tbsps clear honey
90g/3oz wholemeal flour
150g/5oz rolled oats
30g/1oz sesame seeds
1 tsp cinnamon

1. Place the low fat spread in a mixing bowl and cook for 2 minutes on HIGH to melt.

Step 2 Mix the honey and dry ingredients into the melted low fat spread.

2. Mix in the honey and the dry ingredients. Pat the mixture onto a dinner plate which has been covered with greaseproof paper. It should be at least 1.25cm/½ inch thick.

Step 2 Using a rubber spatula or the back of a spoon, press the mixture onto a plate lined with greaseproof paper.

Step 3 Cut the mixture into wedges while still warm, but allow to cool before transferring to a serving plate.

3. Bake for 2½ minutes on HIGH. Cut into 8 wedges while still warm.
4. Leave to cool completely before serving.

Cook's Notes

 TIME: Preparation takes about 10 minutes, and cooking takes 4½ minutes.

! WATCHPOINT: Don't be tempted to sample the flapjacks before they are commpletely cool. The mixture gets very hot and can burn.

 PREPARATION: Be sure to cut the flapjacks before they cool completely, or they will break apart.

 VARIATION: If you don't like the taste of honey, substitute the same quantity of golden syrup.

HOME-MADE YOGHURT

Makes approximately 570ml/1 pint

*Yoghurt made with the help of a microwave oven eliminates the need
for temperature testing and for cleaning messy pans.*

430ml/¾ pint skimmed milk
4 tbsps skimmed milk powder
4 tbsps low fat natural yoghurt

Step 4 Whisk in the milk powder and leave to cool to a hand-hot temperature.

Step 3 Boil the milk until slightly reduced in volume.

1. Put the milk in a large bowl and cook uncovered for 2 minutes on HIGH.

2. Stir and cook for a further 2-3 minutes on HIGH until the milk boils.

3. Reduce the setting and cook uncovered for 8 minutes on DEFROST, stirring occasionally until the milk is slightly reduced in volume.

4. Whisk in the milk powder and leave to cool until comfortable to the touch.

5. Whisk in the yoghurt, then pour into a wide-

necked flask or divide between the glasses in a yogurt maker.

6. Cover and leave for 8 hours until the yoghurt is just set, then refrigerate covered for a further 3-4 hours.

Step 5 Whisk in the yoghurt which is needed as a starter.

Cook's Notes

TIME: Preparation takes about 5 minutes, and cooking takes about 12-13 minutes. Setting time will be about 8 hours.

VARIATION: Flavourings such as fruit, honey, spices, vanilla or chocolate can be added to the yoghurt before it is left to set.

WATCHPOINT: Make sure that the milk mixture has cooled sufficiently before adding the yoghurt, otherwise it will curdle!

WHOLEMEAL BREAD

Makes 1 loaf

Speed up yeast cookery by using your microwave oven. Use it to prove the dough and then bake it in less than half the conventional baking time.

350g/12oz wholemeal flour
120g/4oz plain flour
1 tsp sea salt
280ml/½ pint milk
30g/1oz low fat spread
1 tbsp active dried yeast
1 tsp brown sugar
1 egg, beaten with a pinch of sea salt
Oatmeal or bran (optional)

Step 7 Roll up the dough, seal the ends and place in a loaf pan.

1. Sift the flours and the salt into a large bowl. Make a well in the centre.

2. Heat the milk for 15 seconds on HIGH. Stir in the low fat spread to melt and the yeast to dissolve. Stir in the sugar, and pour this liquid mixture into the well in the dry ingredients. Stir to incorporate all the ingredients gradually.

3. Turn out onto a floured surface, and knead for 10 minutes.

4. Put the dough into a lightly greased bowl and turn over to coat all sides. Cover the dough mixture with cling film or a clean towel. Leave to rise for 1-1½ hours in a warm place.

5. Alternatively, place the bowl of dough in a dish of hot water and put into the microwave oven for 4 minutes on LOW. Leave the dough to stand for 15 minutes and then repeat until the dough has doubled in bulk.

6. Shape the dough by knocking it back and kneading lightly for about 2 minutes.

7. Roll or pull the dough out to a rectangle and then roll up tightly. Seal the ends and tuck under slightly. Put into a lightly greased loaf dish, about 22.5cm x 12.5cm/9 inches x 5 inches.

8. Cover the loaf dish loosely and leave the dough to rise in a warm place for about 30 minutes, or use the microwave rising method.

9. Brush the top of the loaf with lightly beaten egg and sprinkle on the bran or oatmeal, if using. Cook on MEDIUM for 6-8 minutes giving the dish a quarter turn every 1 minute.

10. Increase the temperature to HIGH and cook for 1-2 minutes, rotating as before. The top will spring back when lightly touched when the bread is done.

11. Leave in the dish for 5 minutes before turning out onto a wire rack to cool. If desired, oatmeal or bran may be pressed onto the base and sides of the cooling loaf.

Cook's Notes

TIME: Preparation takes 1-2 hours and cooking takes about 10-12 minutes.

COOK'S TIP: Using the microwave instructions for proving bread dough will cut the time this step usually takes by half.

WATCHPOINT: Yeast will die at too high a temperature, so test the milk and if very hot, allow to cool slightly before adding the yeast.

Index

Edited by Jane Adams and Jillian Stewart
Photography by Peter Barry
Recipes Prepared and Styled for Photography by Bridgeen Deery
and Wendy Devenish
Designed by Claire Leighton, Sally Strugnell and Alison Jewell